SEE

the

WORLD

through

MY EYES

KIERFT NOËL

NEWMAN SPRINGS PUBLISHING
320 Broad Street
Red Bank, NJ 07701

First originally published by Newman
Springs Publishing 2023

ISBN 978-1-63881-899-1 (Paperback)
ISBN 978-1-63881-904-2 (Digital)

Printed in the United States of America

Prisoner of Nostalgia

I find myself with you most of the time
in a place where only you and I dwell
deep inside
the labyrinth of my mind
a secret place,
most sacred belongs to you.
A secret room,
filled with the brightest of lights, love, warmth,
care, and the sweetest smell of your scent.
Such an intoxicating aroma.
I think about you all the time
the secret things that I hide from the world
a prisoner of nostalgia.
The shackles are off, still I remain
cemented in the cell I can't leave.
There's no better place I'd rather be.
Your gratuitous kindness and goodness
penetrated my armor with a single blow
such a skilled warrior
how can I let you go, stay.
I'm a man who has never
been the beneficiary
of one kind of gesture.

Your inspiring nature, words,
and kindness captured my heart.
I am the prisoner of nostalgia
lock me in and bury the key
forever your inmate.
Just me all alone
in the penitentiary that you own.

Surgical

This is an operation of my most sacred being
surgical scalpels are the words
that slice open a piece of me
revealing what lies inside
the chambers of the great pyramids
I bleed gold
my flesh is made of diamonds
my organs are precious gems
I am black excellence.

I Can't Breathe

one statement became a slogan
one slogan became a movement
black lives matter!
thousands of feet on the pavement
marching, screaming, protesting
against the disease coded
in this great nation's DNA!
we are the generation
that must cut the cancer of racism
out of America once and for all
life, liberty, and the pursuit of happiness
a universal law that is guaranteed
to all species under the sun.
racism only exists in the human species
ask yourself, Are we truly the most enlightened
ones in the animal kingdom
or is *Homo sapiens* the least bright?
hate and discrimination have no place
in the jungle, survival, and coexistence
the only thing that matters, here in the
        civilized world all life matters
the foot of racism will no longer be on the necks
of those deem lesser

we, as a nation, must rise and stand firm!
against the injustice of the wicked.
collectively as one
we have to muster the strength, courage
and the light within
to overcome this darkness and the sins of the past
George Floyd stopped breathing
so that we can breathe one breath at a time
our nation will be reborn
inhaling the fresh air
free of the pollution, corruption
and destruction of a racist mind
this is a new day. A new world
this is the birth of a nation
the revolution televised
black, white, Asians, and Spanish
together like a rainbow in the sky
the melting pot of gold.

Expedition

what am I searching for
I've yet to know
the god's eternal clock, life's greatest mystery
under the dark sun
in the blindness of my senses
I see the great pyramids
such wonders
a mystery under the dark moon
the wind blows, swirling
dancing, hand in hand,
with the sand of time
one question reinstates in my frontal lobe
what am I searching for in this cosmic soup of life?

The Perfect Gardener

I am, my mother's troubled seed
millions of sperms race toward
her precious eggs
somehow, I'm the one to cross the finish line
you carried me for nine months
dealt with all the pain and discomfort
the swelling of your feet, the morning sickness
and the weights added to your small frame
the minute you heard my cry
it was pure bliss!
you held me close
close to your heart
a wonder in time
great things you had planned for me
through me, you shall live your dreams
the dreams you sacrificed
your only wish was for this seed
to grow and blossom
in to a tree that reaches
the hands of heaven
transcending the hands of time
but under the sun's scorching heat
environmental disasters

this tree dried up before it flourished
however
the perfect gardener you are
so tender and delicate, caring and loving
taking time every morning
to water a lifeless flower

Dedicated to Lanita, my mother

Celestial Navigation

everything in life is guided by a force
    that can't be explained
celestial navigation
step-by-step, our destiny was written
by the divine
in the stars, our souls intertwine
lost in this cosmic ocean
of peculiar emotions, floating on a raft
watching the sun peek behind the clouds
my passion is like a strong tide
waves of emotions taking me to a place unknown
exploring a side of me, never known to exist
celestial bodies in the midnight sky
nautical astronomy
latitudes, horizons, prime meridians
celestial equator, celestial poles—
North, West, South, East
the coordination to your heaven
is a treasure I will cherish till I perish
lost in the pool of life, like a pirate at sea
I watch the birds play
under the heavens blue dome
wishing it was you and me.

The Hidden Passage

what was hidden from me all along
where my capabilities, abilities
to go beyond all impossibilities
the passage of champions.

The Well

they made a wish
tossing me like coins in a well
to the bottom, I sank, left there to die
in a cold dark hole.
So many have passed judgment upon me
others have forsaken me
a penny in a wishing well
sitting on my tail.
I see the light; the way out is apparent
my thoughts aren't clouded.

One day, I shall climb out this well
and I, too, will toss a coin
to make a wish.

Damn!

A sad little song.
I know you been through a lot
Life was never easy
Wishing you died
The night you lost your baby
I could never understand
The pain that you feel inside
But I could try, I'm that guy
Got a shoulder for you to cry
Life's a bitch, but her sex good
I know pain, and that's all she brings
That's the most real thing
No food plus a broken heart
She went from A1
To who's that with all them track marks
From prom queen
To selling her body in vacant parks
Feeling terrified to hope
Dead inside, to cope with the pain
She shooting dope, arms with no vein—damn!

DAMN!
I told her to get clean, never lose hope
I want to see her be a queen again
She smiled pose for a second
Like its prom again
Saw it in her blue eyes reminiscing
Visions of her better self she was seeing.
Thanking me for treating her like a human being
Not like some junky, she looked me in the eyes
And thank me again for not judging
Told her we all got demons
Nobody's perfect, nobody's an angel
This is from the heart no angle
I said she deserves better, get clean
She playfully said a promise to get clean
If you stop dealing, I said okay I ain't playing
I want to see you winning
Like back in high school a year ago
Not too long ago, you remember
The hottest snow bunny in school
In the middle of December
She laughed and
Said, "For a dealer, you suck, you know
But you right you know
I need rehab, tomorrow promise I'll go"
But tomorrow never came

It's fucked up in the game
Shit got me fucked up in the head
Next day, they found her dead
Strangled by a John she was seeing
All over a couple of bags of crack and heroin
They were fighting—damn!

Damn!
In the afterlife
I hope you found peace
Reunited with your baby living life
I see you through my third eye
And the vision of your smile makes me cry
Danielle, Danielle, Danielle
You're finally free, but damn, I wish
Your freedom didn't come at such a high price
The loss of your life—damn!

IG Model

Girl, it's okay to be you.
Take away the mask.
Let the world see the real you.
All the scars and the wounds,
that's what makes you imperfectly beautiful,
but beautiful nonetheless.
I'm tired of all the stigmas,
associated with what beauty is,
when truthfully what beauty is,
is something that can't be defined,
no words on a blank line.

Ten thousand, she paid for her body.
Couldn't understand it.
Beauty is skin-deep, wish she knew it,
but fuck it.
I played my part in her mental destruction.
I ain't innocent,
helped pay for her surgeries, big-butt obsession,
Tits standing up at attention.
Now she feels beautiful,
when all along she was beautiful.
Complications from the surgeries,

now I'm to blame,
told her not to touch the flame.
She reached, got burned,
now she's scorned,
on my head, she placed a crown of thorn.

Whispers of the Wind

A bitter taste from the sweetest fruit
a darkened night from the brightest day
a drop of tear from a smiling face
in this darkened space
love is a stranger veiled with grace
nights so long
dreams prolonged
visions gone till the early morning
a better tomorrow we hope
praying the next day bring
hear the cage birds sing
whether whatever the storm may bring.

Prayers made and request declined
God is a man we can't define
cruel sometimes
good all the time
the travesty of my holy union
the burden of faith
the wisdom of age
the innocence of children
so young in age
a flower blooms
from the seeds we groom.

A river streams to the ocean blue
a day so gloom
gray as the moon
upon mortals below
the sky witnesses
the whispers of the wind.

Inmate. WII2327

Crucified in the court of man
by those with no reflection
a victim of their moral virtues
your strength helps me
carry the cross a burden
I alone should bear
Mother, don't cry, remain brave
knowledge from the oracle
my destiny is much greater
then a state number
when the time comes, after all the battles
are fought, a soldier in the Lord's army
I will meet fate at the crossroads
embracing the crown she places on my head
the rise of a slave to a king.

The Fountain

The world is a desert, thirst for material gain,
we drink from the fountain of pain,
satisfying the scale of happiness and joy.
Angels and demons,
the rifles of God are constantly aimed,
at the shadows before me.
Overflowing my cup with the waters of agony,
until the day it spills over,
my spirit is forever trap
doing mathematics with the stars.

Public Court

The world is full of spectators
weighing their opinions
angels with no halos
horns protruding
yet they're blind to their true nature.

She's a hoe, she a slut—so what!
she sleeps with a lot of men—so what!
she dressed like a hooker—so what!
she strips at a club—so what!

He's a criminal, he the worst
he's locked up for murder, he evil
he's the devil, he sold drugs
he's the scum of the earth, he gangbang.

What they don't know and don't see
is the brokenness, the loneliness
yet she got a heart full of gold.

What they don't know and don't see
is the brokenness, the loneliness
yet he got a heart bigger than the world.

Spectators and their perceptions
pretending to be flawless
chastising us for our mistakes
how are we supposed to grow then?

Go ahead, let them bang the gavel
satisfy their ego, make themselves feel better
by believing and spreading propaganda
because their truth is much darker.

Broken Clock

Here we go again, sorry this is the end
for the last time all the money spent
can't make the heart happy.
I know I did you wrong, it's plain to see
tears coming down, baby, I'm sorry
sounding like a broken record really.
It was the Hennessy and ecstasy
that had me falling victim to my
      animalistic tendency.
I ain't trying to point the finger but shorty
tempted me, kissing on me
and grabbing my willy.
What you expected, I'm a man.
I'm weak, please forgive me.
I ain't trying to make no excuses, but damn!
Please excuse me.
You promised to always love me
through sickness and health,
and I'm sick mentally, I'm addicted to sex.
No matter the storm, you promised to be here.
Now I don't know it's funny
how one mistake can change your heart
to the point where you change your love for me.

Got me wondering
how much love did you really have for me then?
I know I'm to blame, and it's a shame.
My betrayal got you feeling like lame
got you looking stupid to all your friends, no game.
That was never my intention.

If I could right all the wrongs
change the same old songs
would you still be mine
would you still be mine, would you?

We were meant to be, ain't no question.
When it came to you, ain't no second-guessing.
How can you do me like that
put a knife through my back
all along cheating behind my back?
Said you loved me; I don't understand that.
Did you really mean that
or did you say that, just to say that?
Playing with my heart, mind, and emotions
what happened to trust and devotion
evolution, thinking our love was transforming
evolving, into something, beyond the hands of time.
Had me bragging to my friends all the time
how we growing and progressing

how much we were meant for each other
how you never felt this love for no other.
Yeah, right, I was dumb for believing that.
It's okay, I blame myself for that
middle finger to what you say now
ain't got time for the games now.
The clock's broken
no more crying and stressing.
You broke something that was sacred, trust,
then lied about it.
Now you want forgiveness and trust.
All the money in the world can't buy my love.
You lost me.

Truth

In the secrecy of my heart
looking in the mirrors, I despise what I see
I hate myself, I'm a failure
the shackles of my thoughts
suicidal ideas dancing in my brain
at times, I want to die
see what's on the other side
a rope around the neck squeezes the life out
a bullet to the head scrambles the yoke,
a hot shot to the vein feels no pain
the best way probably
the world won't miss me; it's better without me
I'm nobody
just one in a million black males in jail
I close my eyes and see blood
life's main artery sliced open
the day's loop, can't sleep
nightmares
playing on the widescreen
mental health issues, drugs get abuse
I wear depression like the finest linen
stress hang on my neck, a diamond chain
Cuban links, expensive problems

I hate my life, I hate myself
living in pain, hit by a train
I hear death calling
knocking at my front door but
it's not time to let him in yet
the truth is
I got a bright future, so do you.

Sacrilege

Coke in the Pyrex
the affliction of a pure soul
dirty needles in the bathroom
steam pipes in the kitchen
empty fridge, empty mind
broken school, broken tool
invest in a wall, not the poor.

Monetary Mind

Laws of attraction, my mind race
at a NASCAR pace,
when I'm blunted
thinking about the cream
the grind, how do I elevate
take it to the top floor from the first
right now, what could be worst
my visions clear, paramount view
they say life's a bitch
watch me pimp that hoe like a mack do.

Linden

The leaves flourish with desire
rooted in faith
the commanding forces of mankind.

Main Street

Look at all the hopeless faces
sleeping on the corner
panhandling for a dollar
to ease the hunger, or feed their addiction
can't stay sober, need more liquor
the answer to a life
crumble by earthquakes
their spirit, broken
so misery becomes their master
each and every day, the tunnel darkens
the anchor sinks a little deeper
mental captivity, ain't no escaping
life is a drain, from the eyes
there's no more light in their life
so I break down my last Benjamin
and give them a little piece of my life.

Therapy

When drugs are the only things
That have you on cloud nine—life's sad
And when the drugs are gone, the high wears off
Grounding, in reality, is bleak
Face-to-face with the blemishes
Of my mental chemistry, a class
I rather avoid at all cost
I was thought from the school of hard knock
Black folks don't need therapy, you ain't crazy
Problems you deal with it, learn to live with it
I witnessed a friend die
Blood squirting from his head, still I can't cry
Learned how to live with it, I get high
Smoked weed till my eyes bleed
The tears of a soldier at war
Pop pills till I'm blasted
Out the cannons of my depression
Mind somewhere in the fifth heaven
And still climbing, riding the perfect wave
Aero projecting over the world
I'm on cloud nine, then reality checks in
And it's time to do it all over again
I'm a man of pride
I don't share my feelings or my thoughts
But thank you for listening.

High Rollers

When the casino's open,
all the bets are in,
it's left in the hands of luck,
who lose or win,
roll the dice, pray for luck.

When the casino's open,
the cards get dealt,
if your hand is too good to fold,
double down on your bet,
risk it all, be bold!

When the casino's open,
the wheels are spun,
black and red, the colors mix,
Russian roulette, the revolver sing,
one-shot bang, the bullet kisses.

When the casino's open,
I gamble with my life,
the most precious prize,
poker face, cut deep as a knife,
ambitious, nothing to lose, look in my eyes.

Women

when the seasons change
from summer to winter, and the leaves fall
still, you remain green like the budding of spring.

you are the voice of duty
the intelligent orientation to life
unlimited in your love like waters in the seven seas.

you are nature's gift to a world so strange
the appetite of the gods and angels
the making of the stars and galaxies.

this world is a damaged place and unforgiving
so unfortunately, your worth
goes unnoticed until it's beneficial.

The Cabin

A million little pieces scattered
on the wooden floor, reflecting
the firelight in an obscure way
as smoke escapes the kissing lips
of the chimney into the winter sky
through the window frames
smooth like a cat burglar
she sneaks her way in
extending her arms to me
erecting goose bumps on the skin.

Naked on the wooden floor the pieces lay
as I gather my thoughts
coffee and whiskey ménage in the cup I hold
the holy matrimony is somewhat maudlin
as I battle the chilling breeze.

The sweet smell of burned woods
invades my nostril while mellifluously
music of old soul play. I dance
without a care in the world hugging my cup
like I haven't seen her in years.

When the winter strikes, I retreat
to the lonely cabin in the woods
away from the troops of my adversary
the one strategic move of a general
with no pawns, stuck in a game of chess.

Every so often the bears visit
melodramatic in their approach
looking for a prey, their meal ticket
packs of wolves circle the place
but I'm no prey, a predator of the highest degree.

A million little pieces scattered on the
wooden floor, reflecting the firelight
in an obscure way. mesmerized
by the patterns I see, time moves at a different
speed in this cabin.

Two little fingers point the way
the time of days past
million little pieces each one so delicate
and valuable to the bigger picture of things
piece by piece, I gather the broken pieces.

In a box they go, the broken pieces
on the skin of the box
I tattoo the words *fragile and delicate*
please handle with care, do not drop!
inside is a broken object of great value.

Smoke escapes the kissing lips of the chimney
into the bright summer morning sky
a package arrives at the door
with the look of familiarity
on it, in bold letters is written
fragile and delicate, please handle
      with care, do not drop!
inside is an object of great value.

Gently, I open the box
there inside is a beating heart
with a small note that reads
the beginning is the end
and the end is the beginning
time waits for no one
in the cabin.

See the World through My Eyes

See the world through my eyes

See the world through my eyes
so cynical, dimmed like the morning sun
soever happy as the graveyards
where dreams are made.

See the world through my eyes
where Lady Justice is no longer asleep
where her sword is only raised against the rich
where the Libra scale ain't broken
    weighing the heart of men.

See the world through my eyes
where our mothers are on a pedestal
where women are valued and respected
    as the gatekeepers of life
where women are not demoralized,
    sexualized, and demonized.

See the world through my eyes
where religious moral principles
don't conflict with the principles of love.
where holy men of God don't violate our children
where darkness lives in the light.

See the world through my eyes
where God lives among men
where Lucifer repents for the sins of his pride
where holiness is foolishness.

See the world through my eyes
where everyone is color-blind
where wars are forbidden
where the government tells no lies.

See the world through my eyes
where religion is dead
where everyone lives godlike
what a peaceful world.

See the world through my eyes
so cynical, dimmed like the moon
in the midnight sky
soever happy as the graveyards
where dreams are made.

Blind Love

In search of love she looks
in all the wrong places, dark space
mentally impaired blind to her lineage
of a queen's race.
Her crown made of the finest gold
her soul divine, a goddess among mortals
but she lacks the proper knowledge to understand
can't fault her, years of abuse, and degradation.
Her worth she can't comprehend
pleasing others, she fails to please herself
mental kamikaze she hates herself
freely, sharing her God-given treasure
to bring others pleasure, no matter the measure.
Thinking a man will validate her worth
she just wants to be loved
blind to real love, the love of self.

Coldest Winter

The coldest winter ever
is the death of a star,
snowflakes cover the grave
cold breeze through the bone
make the soul shiver
falling on naked trees the snow lay
bird migration to the south
leaves the sky empty and boring
cloud shapes bring memories of old
a perfect circle the sun
heating the atmosphere somewhat
winter storms, battles of the heaven
mortals, victims of the aftermath
the forces of the wind
the showers of snow, so white and pure
frozen in time, some forever lives
the coldest winter ever, ever
is the death of a star
shooting through the midnight sky.

Time bomb
life's complex when it comes to affairs of the heart
my insecurities like a minefield
bombs buried underneath the surface
the cause of my paralyzed state of mind
I love hard, a curse that some are blessed with
I get lost in my feelings, the passion,
        the intensity, the romance
the waves of emotions are like a high I hate chasing
still every now and then, I hear the needle calling
the bomb ticking, counting down ever so gently
3, 2, 1—boom!

Hendrix

These are the strings of my life
Steady getting pulled by the fingers of the world
The music of life, my life is but a note in time
I alone should play.

Where I'm at
I'm in a space of mental despair
I never knew the ills of life
till I became of age
handcuffs tightening
over life I love and hate.
My adolescence stolen at a young age
I was forced to grow up and be a man
nothing can ever prepare a person
for the destructions that life throws at you.
At times, the darkness consumes me
interlocking hands with my soul
oppressed and depressed
my energy diminishes
vanishing, like steam from a boiling pot
when I sit back and reflect
on where I'm at in life.
The vehicle of my destiny

steadily on a crash course.
The tidal waves of pessimism
suffocates, holding me under
each time a little longer and longer.
Still, I must rise above what is
out of the ashes, the phoenix rose
so will I
rebirth, in the flames of my misery.

Fear
Fear is like seeds planted in a nurtured soil
watered in a timely fashion
with the right amount of sunlight
it grows and grows until it's rooted deeply.
We are all afraid when it comes to affairs of the heart
Some a little less, some a little more.
But I'm not afraid to confess the sins of my heart.
I am afraid of love, afraid of the destruction
it may bring mentally, physically, and emotionally.
Why do we torture ourselves in the name of love?
I fail to understand human nature
perhaps it's my nature that I've yet to understand.
For they say, living a life in fear is
      worse than death itself.

Outcast
I'm lost why do I feel guilty
about not caring for the things
I once was cared for before
street shit and scandalous friends.
I don't care
for a lot of shit no more.
Mostly
I'm just done with the bullshit.
But I hate
that I feel like an outcast for that
clashing with the swords of what
I evolved out of. Really
all I care about is getting my life back.
I don't want to fail before I try.
I don't want broken wings before I fly.
I want the house, the cars, and a loving family
I want the simple shit
without feeling content with the
    little shit. Make sense?
I don't want fame, and I don't want a lot of money.
I just want enough to take care of my loved ones.
I want a nice beer and cookouts with the family.
I want real change and growth.
Just because you moving different
doesn't mean you're elevating maybe.

Just because I'm feeling different
about some things doesn't mean that I'm growing.
I don't know. Just know what I want
and if I have to distance myself
to obtain what I want
then fuck it!
I'll be an outcast.

Pain
As I wipe the blood from my wounds
my heart leaks, blood flows.
How can one patch a wound that's internal?
Sometimes, I cry, but that's only in the dark
away from the world to see
away from the judgment of society
soever judging you and I.
A secret I keep to myself.
All I know is abandonment and pain.
How can I be happy?
Still, life goes on, moving carefree.
May my pain bring you joy.
Don't be afraid, smile for me.

The space between us
Only when the light is gone
and my world darkens like the deepest

part of the ocean blue, do I see you.
In the darkness, I hold you.
This moment in time, I wish to never let go
but when the sun rises and the birds sing
we part ways like a one-night fling
'till the stars and the moon dance again.
If only I could close the space between us
for just a second in time
I would partake on a journey like Dante's *Inferno*.
Like stardust sprinkled down from
      the highest heavens
paradise the new Garden of Eden.
This forbidden fruit our passion
so ever growing from a cub to a lion
no matter the distance
in Godspeed, my love travels
with the resemblance of Hermes upon its arrival.

Medicine
Heroin, heroin, heroin
my soul is forever in your possession
a slave to the instant cosmic feelings of ecstasy
when we are one.
I crave your passion
your soft lips, your tender kisses
and the smell of your body.

The cure to my sickness
I need you, I want you, I must have you
in the worst of ways, by any means.
Our fatal attraction is deadly
but you're my soul mate.
My body aches without your touch
sitting on the couch, deep in my slumber
stress and depression, I meditate on you
of all things under the sun
why must my obsession be you
I hate you.

Broken mirrors
Out the divine light arrays
illuminating the deepest
corners of the abyss.

Internal departure from the demons within
not long ago I couldn't recognize
the person I was
the mirror reflecting a stranger within.

Crows appear from the cracks of shattered dreams
piece by piece they take shape
manifesting, shaping the pieces of glass
till they fly neurotically in search of water.

Passing through the portals of life and death
the cycle of God's eternal wheel.
infinite wisdom is the price for pain
this of course is done in vain

Condemned by the morals of others
our life is stained
we live to die, what's really here to gain.

Acid trip
The wind sleeps on me
the desert ground cracks beneath my feet
the ocean swallows my emotions
unmoved by the moon in the sky.
The fire burns within my heart
my passion flames like the suns in the galaxy.
The water runs deep, through my veins
cleansing me of all impurities.
The dirt covers my body
like paints on a canvas.
The universe speaks to me
granting me access to its inner matrix.
The stars in the midnight sky
direct my path to Sheol.

In Time

In time, the train of thought will change
derailed from its course
unto a track of progressive ideology.
A theory I hope to be true
biopsychosocial changes the social
      conditions, redefines a man.
Negative influence breeds a state of mind
destructive to society, destructive behaviors
the expectations of such fetus predictable
psychosocial dwarfism
isolated in the prison of poverty
emotionally deprived, our youths die!
Robbed of a healthy childhood
how can they love
when they don't know what love is.
How can they be a father
when they never had a father?
How can a woman not be broken
when all she knows is abuse?
Rome wasn't built in a day, it took time.
Learning how to love yourself
well, that takes time.

World Stage

When God speaks, the world shakes
shifting the social architecture
dismantling dominance.
The functions of oppression
modern trends, social movements
give voice to the hopeless, the voiceless
producing change with a science.
It's clear the experiments of elitism
the preservation of control and power
for one to rise, another must fall
for dominance, another must submit.
The submission of the mass mind
gives power to the policies of the wicked.

Embrace Me

embrace me
do not reject me
hold me and protect me
embrace my love
weight my heart upon the Libra scale
if you're in need of clarity
naked like a newborn
truest in my purest form
my love is unmeasurable
hold me, love me
accept me
as I am
flawed!
embrace me
do not reject me
see me
through your eyes
not the eyes of others
see me
I am, who I am
what I am
imperfectly
molded

by the hands
of the invisible one
neither time nor space
can ever erase
the masterful artwork
that we create
hold me, love me
embrace me
do not reject
the
purest part of me.

Prison Cell

In my prison cell
I fight with the walls, kicking and punching
Until my hands are bruised up, swollen
And bones are broken, still, I fight the fight.

In my prison cell
I talk to the walls, and they talk back
Conversations deep like the ocean blue
That harbors life yet to be discovered.

In my prison cell
I make love to the walls, endorphins rushing
Oxytocin and dopamine released
The cause of my mental pregnancy.

In my prison cell
I silent the walls adjusting their volume
They stare, looking in awe
Questioning the foundation on which they stand.

In my prison cell
In the solitude of my thoughts
Comes life.

Jesus of Lübeck

Baptized by Christianity
Jesus of Lübeck
stolen, bound, shipped
castrated, raped, and killed
force to sleep on the oceanic plates
food for the life that occupies
such colonies and states.
The sins witnessed by the sea
only if they could speak
lynched from trees rebels
my forefathers and mothers.
The revolution lives on
armed with the best weapon
stolen from its hidden place
committing mental robbery.
We must fight back, clap back
beating in my chest is a panther's heart.

Eardrum Ecstasy

Your voice tastes like strawberry cheesecakes
like strawberry dipped in chocolate
like ice cream and vanilla whipped cream
the cause of explosions in one's kingdom
your heavenly flavor attacking and battling
the tastebuds when my ears get a taste of you.
Hello, hey, the beginning words to mental orgasm
eardrum ecstasy, molly water
the tangling feelings coursing through the body
taking my spirit to the highest peaks of mountains
paramount view, spiritual awakening
connecting to a higher power
when the phone rings, and you answer—hello.

FTW

Fuck the world
the people with the most sin
are the ones to cast the first stone
Fuck the world
the ones with the evilest in their hearts
are the ones judging—hypocrites!
Fuck the world
Fuck you too, if you ever judge me
take a look in the mirror, that's who you judge.

Family

Family are not the ones with blood ties
family is the people that prove
where their loyalty lies
when the mountain of impossibilities
needs to be a climb, and they climb it with you.
In my blackened eyes, blood doesn't make us family
the ones with blood ties are always the first
to untie the strings of relation
when the prism of light doesn't reach
to your end of the tunnel.
Family, who are they
blood relations hold no weight to me.
Cain killed Abel in the Bible
all the fake love and pretend loyalties
secretly thinking the worst of me.
Yeah, family…
The only family I recognize
is not the one I was born in.
My family is the one that struggles created.

Hood Tales

In the hood, some hustle, rap, or play ball
the common denominator we all trying to ball
before the time runs out on the shot clock
violation in the courts of America.
One must discover what their God-given talent is
you just might be the equivalent
to what fifty-two thousand bricks is
Jean-Michel Basquiat in the eighties
masterpiece! This is where greatness lives
born without a penny, still, we make dollars
out of what is
genius minds, don't know what school is
swimming with the fishes come visit
where the mermaids live.
Still trying to find where the American dream is.
Is it in the suburbs with the white picket fences
where kids get high and hate their parents
or is it in my part of town
where them kids come and cop
steal food out of stop and shop for a bag
where a thousand liquor store is.
Where is the American dream? I'm still looking
praying for a palm itch

get money and move on out this ditch
where we watch fiends in backblocks
sucking cocks for some crack rocks
shootings nonstop in the name of respect
where the law is corrupt in every aspect
welcome to the hood, my hood, your hood
is where the mermaids live.

The Ballad of a Fool

The Story of Alexis

THIS IS THE BALLAD OF A FOOL,
THE BALLAD OF A FOOL

Sometimes I think about Alexis
she was one of my exes
Chiquita bonita, used to tell her I love her
but really back then, I was in love with another her
my other girl kept me fly
pocket full of money no lie
creeping on the low
phone ring ignored the call, but I texted, "Hey"
no disrespect, it's true what they say
women intuition, Alexis always calls
when I'm with my side hoe
no time to talk though
I be digging this bitch out like I'm
        trying to find gold
only God knows, what she'll do to you, she a cougar
she deadly like shells ejaculating out the rugger
toxic, still I love her, lost my virginity to her
twelve years old, I became obsessed with her

every day, I had to see her
she fucked my friends too
she had us run a train on her
big pipe, small pipe, she needs an army to satisfy her
young men who she goes after, can't judge her
she's plenty of things, but I don't disrespect my elder.

THIS IS THE BALLAD OF A FOOL,
THE BALLAD OF A FOOL

Alexis but she goes by Lexis
was nothing like my first love, I met her
one day going to the doctor
she was my uber driver
young pretty thing, she went to
     school to be a doctor
she taught me things about the female body
so in turn, I became her doctor
physical inspection, climaxing
eyes rolling, body shaking like the exorcism
she fell in love with my sex
told her, "I ain't the type, you know"
the relationship type, I really don't do the wifely type
she said, "Boy, please,
I don't have the time, plus you ain't my type
this is only a friend plus type of vibe"

I'm like cool, I'm with it
Lexis was Dominican and Haitian
Five six, honey, toned complexion
eventually, she caught feelings
after a couple of sessions, all night sexing
I be eating like I'm lunching
explored her body like Columbus
doing some savage things
till she's left walking like a penguin
she loved my style
"Alexis, please," I pleaded
"don't love me in that way
let's keep it platonic
friends only, I think its best that way"
but it's easier said than done, "Lexis,
        I'm on my way."

THIS IS THE BALLAD OF A FOOL,
THE BALLAD OF A FOOL

My cougar chic started bugging now
talking I didn't spend enough time with her now
I'm acting different 'cause I got me
        a little girlfriend now
I told her, "Don't start tripping now
that shit a turn off, plus you should already know

you the one I'm in love with from the go
no matter what you do to me I always forgive you
when I'm with her, I think of you
every time I kiss her, I picture you"
I assured her can't no chic take your
        place in this world
you took me in and loved me
when nobody gave a fuck about me in this world
you cleaned me up, showed me how to dress
you gave me my style, and you put
        money in my pocket
even though I had to sleep with you, it's all cool
you made me and
I love you, for that, I'm forever in your pocket
when I'm with you, and Alexis calls, I don't answer
I keep everything about you a secret from her
you're my hidden pleasure
nobody know me like you do
all the orgies we been in
tagging all my friends in
plus all the other bitches
from around the way you helped me get in
fuck them, then dissed them
all the games you gave me, you showed me
that scandalous bitches ain't nothing like them
they attack when they sense weakness

play with a man's heart, leave them
    spineless, penniless
you even made me witness
how these bitches will have dudes
feeling like they the one
something like Ne-Yo in the matrix
only to find out at the end of the movie
there are other Ne-Yos in her matrix
you even showed me how
some women use sex as a weapon
and how to reverse it, use my sex like a weapon
my former rightness teacher
you taught me things that take years to master
in return, you left me emotionally scarred
still you, my baby, I love you dearly.

THIS IS THE BALLAD OF A FOOL,
THE BALLAD OF A FOOL

I was blind, but Alexis saw the good in me
told me I got a good heart, and my essence heavenly
I teased that I'm more like a scout for the other side
she started getting nosy asking what I do for money
I told her I'm gigolo, she laughed playfully
Lexis told me the story of how her mom OD'd,
from a bag of heroin mixed with fetty

at least she ain't feel no pain the irony
she said somberly
she stated she hate drug dealers, they the worst
they selling poison for money
I said, "Girl, don't judge nobody."
        She said, "I beg to differ
dealers are live walking Lucifer"
I avoided her question that night, I don't want to lie
but I will if I must, I don't want to see her cry
months went by, no more questions
on how I make a living
till one day, she stopped at my house unexpectedly
she caught my friend and Madonna dancing
damn, now I wish I never gave her that key
anyways, she called me, ignored the call
I was with my cougar hoe
focused on pleasing her I need now,
my stash kind of light. Lexis started chain texting
in all capital, "We need to talk"
letting me know she mad, I replied
"I'll be at the crib from where I'm
        at. It's a 30-second walk"
she texted back, "I'll be waiting"
soon as I got to the house, Lexis started screaming
the fire in her eyes, she turned red like a white girl
she asked, "Kierft! Do you sell drugs?"

I'm thinking, *Damn, my baby girl*
I thought about lies, but that felt wrong
I said, "Yes, I do," and I still felt wrong
so much going on, I tried to explain
Alexis slapped me then stormed out
I ran after Lexis, calling her name out
pleading my case like, "Let's talk this out"
I caught her by the car, she crying making a scene
neighbors in their windows, watching the scene
ready to call 911
she slapped me again, this time with more power
that's when I grabbed her, told her I loved her
she put her head in my chest, tears on my chest
I know she heard my heart skip a beat
so she knows it's real
tears flowing down her pretty face
that's something I hate for real.
Lexis took a deep breath, exhaled looking at the sky
then she looked me deep in the eye
        and said she pregnant
I was real ignorant
I blurted out stupidly, "Is it mine?"
she gave me a crazy look like, "Boy, you out of line"
deep down I knew the answer, she spoke softly
"Kierft, if you really love me, stop slinging really
fuck your friends, all you need is me

the streets don't love you"
I was a fool then. I told her, "I knew them
before I ever knew you
we from the same block, can't turn
     my back on them"
that ain't real boo
Lexis quickly slapped me again and screamed
"Real is being there for me and your kid
instead of being dead or in prison doing a bid!"

THIS IS THE BALLAD OF A FOOL,
THE BALLAD OF A FOOL

After Alexis slapped me for like the third time
she got in her car, slammed the door
I watched her flip me the finger then back out
thinking damn shorty really spazzing out
this cougar chick left me emotionally damaged
I start thinking, *Fuck, Lexis, trying to use leverage*
giving me an ultimatum, fuck wrong with that bitch
you know the games these females play
I woke up the next day, around midday
lit a blunt, started smoking
nonstop, my phone kept ringing,
     It was Ashley calling

Alexis's best friend, a white girl with
        different hair color
every time I see her
she said that's her way of self-expressing
she always rocking uggs and legging
anyways, she started rambling
talk real fast, telling me what happened
"Last night, Lexis got into a car accident
a real bad one
she was speeding couple of blocks from your street
J whatever, yeah, that one
when she smashed full force
into a car, backing out to the street
another car hit her on the side too
they had to get the jaws of life too
she in a coma, doctors said lucky to be alive too
but the baby she lost it, boo
doctors say she can never have kids now too"
I felt a pain deep in my chest
got on my knees, prayed to God
        she makes it through
months went by, and Lexis healed up
I was by her side every night till the sunup
when she was comatose, now she's up
she told me she hates me forever
said I broke her heart

I wasn't man enough to choose her
the streets who I chose.

THIS IS THE BALLAD OF A FOOL,
THE BALLAD OF A FOOL

Alexis, I was a fool then, can't pretend
I was a little boy then
that was trying to act like a grown man
I blame myself for everything
I promised you that I was nothing like them
but yet I turned out to be, the worst of them
hate the fact that I'm the cause of your acid tears
misery loves company, I left you scarred for years
robbed you of motherhood
the growing of a fetus inside of you
an experience you well deserve
life through you a curve
pitched by my hand—damn!
I never knew what love is till now
I know it's too late now, for real now
I'm sitting lonely in a cell, writing this ballad
thinking about everything you told me now
no excuse, but that cougar bitch had a hold on me
I used to crave her passion, but I'm
        done with her now

Lexis, if you ever read these words
feel these words
from the purest chambers of my soul
I'm sorry, please forgive me
I'm not a kid no more, so as a man
I apologize

This the ballad of a fool, the ballad of a fool

A THUG'S PSALM

This the scriptures of a thug
sacred words written by David
trap inside a cave
if you never had to eat around
the molds on a piece of bread
survived on noodles
then you can't feel this
but try to relate, visualize
I was birthed in the fire
where even demons cry
shedding tears that reach
the heavens high
colossal sins I witnessed inside
the walls and confinement of a church
grieving silently
so much weight on my shoulders
still, I stand tall and strong
slave blood runs through my veins
my problem's only a fraction of their pain
still, they remained. So it's a most I maintain
at times I say the Lord's name in vain

no blasphemy, sometimes I just question things
crack smoke clouds the hood, making us insane
melting cocaine, dealt to us
by the hands of the government
destroying generations, poor schools
if one escapes the trap, he's a good boy
Obama's nothing like those niggas
but no matter how far the distance
some still view him as a nigger.
"I'm never. ignorant. getting. goals. accomplished"
like Tupac Shakur once said,
"But I'm not a nigga or nigger
knowledge made my star burn brighter,
I'm a god, erased knowledge burned,
and stolen in ALEXANDRIA.
I'm thugging till my casket drops
no, not destroying my community
I'm shining a light on my people
about the. hate. you. give."
genetically enhancing the generations to come
that's how we beat the cancer of racism
and inequalities
this is a thug's psalm, righteous in heart
but sin at times in mind.

take my hands
I ripped my heart out just to watch it beat
clutching my fist.
I ripped my eyes out just to see the world
through empty sockets.
I slept in coffins just to wake up dead to the world
unfazed by the problems of society.

death is the end to the misery
the beginning to eternity
come, take my hands, and dance
    in the stars with me.

our essence convulsively erupting like volcanoes
among the cosmos.

Golden Eyes

Tears of gold escapes
from her golden eyes
satisfying the thirst of mankind.
With each and every drop
she transforms a mortal
a peasant into a Pharaoh.

Friends

The dynamics of our relationship
is the inner mechanics
that keeps my ship
afloat.

Connections

I feel their pain
mercilessly attacked by
the destroying forces in their world
the dark matter of their universe
the impacts of a bullet penetrating their flesh
the slicing of a knife, cutting
through the elasticity of their skin.
However, nothing compares to the magic potions
of poisonous words
sprayed out the fangs of a walking cobra
intensely infecting the souls
of the minds, it corrupts, like vultures
feasting, it eats away a portion of their spirit.
I hear their cries in the dark
the tears that escape their eyes
stain my cheeks.
I hear the thoughts of suicide.
No, please, don't! There lies the disconnect.
Still every now and then, we connect
link up at the house on the hill
the one with the missing roof
just two old friends, smoking marijuana
eating a bag of Cheetos.

The Poet

The spirit of old speaks through me
writing words, forming sentences
with philosophical views
I'm not Kierft, I am the poet
my fingers play with his brain
like tunes on a piano
I sketch pictures in his mind
add verbs and nouns to his lips
metaphors and similes
I make him speak symbolically
I bring passion to his heart
I help him become a locksmith with words
trapping his emotions and feelings
inside the lines that he writes
I help him decipher the ancient codes
what are the ancient codes?
a secret that can't be told
it's on you to figure it out
and take the time to decipher
look within
channel your inner me
come and visit where the poet lives
who am I?

I have no name
yet my name holds power
I dwell in the souls of men
carrying with me the greater keys of Solomon
and when this vessel's gone, back to the ether
waiting for his turn on the wheels of reincarnation
I will move on and choose another host
that's dwelling in pain, in need of clarity
to life's greatest mystery
I see life through a different lens
I am—the poet.

In This Madness

I smoke blunts in this madness
Help me stress less
I'm a mess, still, I play chess
Queen's gambit legendary move
No one can take my queen place
That's a no, no
Haters know their place that's behind me
I'm coming in the first place, boots laced
Fuck, second place
It ain't an option, ain't no options
It's sink or swim for certain
Like a dolphin, I'm swimming in this ocean
Go hard or go home, I'm an orphan
There's no going back, the world's a kingdom,
And I'm Alexander the Great, welcome

Man-Child

A mental turtle to the virtues of life
Vicariously blin to the life my actions breed
Selfish in my thought process
The burning star of the world
How wrong was I
The small close mind of a man-child
Old in age, but young in mind
The vicissitude in the state of mind
Of a man-child is somewhat spiritual
The illumination of a mind that was once
A resident in the state of triple darkness.

Black Widow

Her seductive venom
Hit the main artery
Manipulating him to be captured
In her web of lies
There, the process of death began.

Blue Smoke

She used to be my light, now I live in the dark
using lead, trying to get me a spark
trying to light me a flame
got to burn through the pain
shelter my heart from these lames.

When the smoke clears
the love ain't the same
they adjusting their aim
so-called brothers, trying to kill me like Cain
they throwing dirt on my grave
ignoring my tears, facing my fears
I have to fight through the tears.

Great Teachers

teach the blind to see
the deaths to listen
and the mutes to talk
great teachers
teach a rock to walk
the dead to live
and the fishes to sing
like Jesus of Nazareth
all great teachers
perform miracles

Dedicated to Hilary Binda

Rated R

As I look outside my window
I see beauty and pain, walking hand in hand
in my neighbor's window
on repeat, the same movie plays over and over again
the husband comes home and attacks
     his old lady once more
the ocean escaping her eyelids, polluting her face
Her bruises, she massages under a cold shower
every Sunday, they prepare once
     more to go to church
Pray for forgiveness and feel the holy spirit's power
every week, the same prayer the wife recites
dear God, please make him stop, soften his hand
Holy Mary mother of God, please
     make him understand.

Is it better to live a life of abuse than a loveless life
to endure physical pain for the sake of the heart.

every Sunday, like a hawk hunting for its prey
I watch the relief and joy on her face
only to have sadness and pain displayed on Monday
I watch like a pigeon, perched upon a
    light pole in my secret place
observing, watching, the sand of time
    diminished day by day.

Sinful

sinful, yes, I am
I'm only human
just like you
one day, we must die
decay in the dirt to bring new life
who shall cast the first stone?
when the God of Jacob starts to read
chapters in the book of life.
We all sin somehow, someway
that's human life
but the greatest sin of all besides blasphemy
is thinking that you're better than me.

About the Author

Kierft Noël's book is only half written. He is an advocate and a member of the Drop LWOP New England Project. He strongly believes that it's not where a person starts in life but where they finish that truly matters. Who we truly are as human beings is so much more than the identities that people in society impose upon us. Kierft is currently incarcerated at this time in Souza-Baranowski maximum-security prison awaiting his appeal. Follow him on IG (Legacy509Lyfe) and Facebook (Kierft Noel). However, the fastest way to contact him directly is through email at corrlinks. com ID no. w112327.

Printed in the USA
CPSIA information can be obtained
at www.ICGtesting.com
LVHW041507311223
767720LV00062B/1644